I LIVE WITH A LEARNING DISABILITY

WRITTEN BY CHRISTINA EARLEY

ILLUSTRATED BY
AMANDA HUDSON

A Starfish Book
SEAHORSE
PUBLISHING

Teaching Tips for Caregivers:

As a caregiver, you can help your child succeed in school by giving them a strong foundation in language and literacy skills and a desire to learn to read.

This book helps children grow by letting them practice reading skills.

Reading for pleasure and interest will help your child to develop reading skills and will give your child the opportunity to practice these skills in meaningful ways.

- Encourage your child to read on her own at home
- Encourage your child to practice reading aloud
- Encourage activities that require reading
- Establish a reading time
- Talk with your child
- Give your child writing materials

Teaching Tips for Teachers:

Research shows that one of the best ways for students to learn a new topic is to read about it.

Before Reading

- Read the "Words to Know" and discuss the meaning of each word.
- Read the back cover to see what the book is about.

During Reading

- When a student gets to a word that is unknown, ask them to look at the rest of the sentence to find clues to help with the meaning of the unknown word.
- Ask the student to write down any pages of the book that were confusing to them.

After Reading

- Discuss the main idea of the book.
- Ask students to give one detail that they learned in the book by showing a text dependent answer from the book.

TABLE OF CONTENTS

I Live with a Learning Disability

Hi! My name is Avi. I am eight years old.

I live with my dad and older sister Mabel. Oreo is my cat.

I was born with a learning **disability**.

Reading is tricky because the letters seem to move around. Writing and spelling are hard, too.

A learning disability is a **condition** of the brain. It affects the brain's **ability** to learn.

Some people with learning disabilities have a hard time with reading, writing, or math. Remembering things and paying attention are difficult for others.

I ride the bus to school. I sit with my friend Ryan.

We talk about our favorite
football teams.

Miss Summer helps me with my reading and spelling. I go to her room with my friend Jo.

My favorite subject is math. It helps me when Mr. Ono reads word problems out loud.

Spelling is **challenging**. I say the
word, say and write each letter,
and then read the word.

Writing is easier when I talk to a computer. It shows me the words as I speak.

I like **inventing** and building things with my dad.

I hope that one of my inventions is
used by everyone around the world!

LEARN ABOUT LEARNING DISABILITIES

What Is a Learning Disability?

A learning disability is a lifelong brain disorder. Even though people with learning disabilities have normal intelligence, they might have trouble understanding or using spoken or written language, doing mathematical calculations, coordinating movements, or directing their attention. Sometimes, learning disabilities are called "hidden disabilities" because they aren't easy to see.

There are different types of learning disabilities. Dyscalculia affects a person's ability to understand numbers and learn math facts. Dysgraphia affects a person's handwriting and fine-motor skills. Dyslexia affects reading and language-based processing skills. Those with nonverbal learning disabilities have trouble interpreting nonverbal cues, such as facial expressions and body language.

People with learning disabilities face challenges. However, with good support and interventions, they can be successful at school, at work, in relationships, and in their communities.

Websites to Visit

International Dyslexia Association: dyslexiaida.org

LD OnLine: ldonline.org

Learning Disabilities Association of America: ldaamerica.org

National Center for Learning Disabilities: ncld.org

Smart Kids with Learning Disabilities: smartkidswithld.org

Take the Pledge for Inclusion

- ☑ I accept people of all abilities.

- ☑ I respect others and act with kindness and compassion.

- ☑ I include people with special needs and disabilities in my school and in my community.

Get your parent's permission to sign the online pledge at PledgeforInclusion.org.

Famous People with Learning Disabilities

Richard Branson: Billionaire

Thomas Edison: Inventor

Keira Knightley: Actor

Jamie Oliver: Chef

Steven Spielberg: Filmmaker

Tim Tebow: NFL player

Thomas Edison

Steven Spielberg

Celebrate and Educate

Learning Disabilities Awareness Month happens in October.

Dyslexia Awareness Month happens in October.

Inclusive Schools Week is the first full week in December.

WORDS TO KNOW

ability (uh-BIL-i-tee): the power to do something

challenging (CHAL-in-jing): hard to do

condition (kuhn-DISH-uhn): a medical problem that lasts for a long time

disability (dis-uh-BIL-i-tee): not able to do something, or not able to do something the way that others can, because of a condition

inventing (in-VEN-ting): thinking up and creating something new

INDEX

COMPREHENSION QUESTIONS

1. Avi has trouble with ___.

   a. reading

   b. hopping

   c. talking

2. A learning disability is a condition of the ___.

   a. muscles

   b. skeleton

   c. brain

3. What does Avi use to help with writing?

   a. a computer

   b. a desk

   c. a ball

4. True or False: People with a learning disability are smart.

5. True or False: Spelling is easy for Avi.

Answers: 1. a, 2. c, 3. a, 4. True, 5. False

ABOUT THE AUTHOR

Christina Earley lives in sunny south Florida with her son, husband, and rescue dog. She has been teaching children with special needs for over 25 years. She loves to bake cookies, read books about animals, and ride roller coasters.

Written by: Christina Earley
Illustrated by: Amanda Hudson
Design by: Under the Oaks Media
Editor: Kim Thompson

Photos: LOC: p. 21 (Thomas Edison); Fred Duval/Shutterstock: p. 21 (Steven Spielberg)

Library of Congress PCN Data
I Live with a Learning Disability /Christina Earley
I Live With
ISBN 979-8-8873-5346-3(hard cover)
ISBN 979-8-8873-5431-6(paperback)
ISBN 979-8-8873-5516-0(EPUB)
ISBN 979-8-8873-5601-3(eBook)
Library of Congress Control Number: 2022948981

Printed in the United States of America.

Seahorse Publishing Company

www.seahorsepub.com

Published in the United States
Seahorse Publishing
PO Box 771325
Coral Springs, FL 33077